TRAINS

First published in Great Britain by
CAXTON EDITIONS
an imprint of
The Caxton Book Company,
16 Connaught Street,
Marble Arch, London, W2 2AF.

ISBN 1 84067 024 X

A copy of the CIP data for this book is available from the British Library upon request.

With grateful thanks to Helen Courtney

Created and produced for Caxton Editions by
FLAME TREE PUBLISHING
a part of The Foundry Creative Media Company Ltd,
Crabtree Hall, Crabtree Lane,
Fulham, London, SW6 6TY.

Printed and bound in Singapore

HEADstart

TRAINS

*The History and the
Magic, Explained
in Glorious Colour*

KAREN SULLIVAN

CE

CAXTON EDITIONS

◄ Contents ►

What is a Train?

A train is a vehicle, or series of vehicles, that runs on a railway. Trains are pulled or pushed by a 'locomotive' (engine), or move by themselves along a railway, which is a track that both carries and guides trains along it.

Trains and railways have been used since ancient times: early civilizations created railways cut out of stone to guide their vehicles.

The first trains were built for use in mines, factory complexes or other industries. These trains were usually powered by people who pushed or pulled them along the tracks, and were widely in use by the sixteenth century. By the nineteenth century railways were considered to be the main symbol of the new industrial age.

Trains were first moved by people, and then by horses or mules, but by the nineteenth century, steam locomotives were used. As trains grew longer and heavier locomotives did too, so that they would have enough power to pull them. One of the first locomotives, the tiny Tom Thumb, built in 1830, had one horsepower (which means the speed and power of one horse), while later trains, such as the American Union Pacific 'Big Boys' built in the 1940s weighed about 400 tons, with 7,000 horsepower.

In the early twentieth century, electric locomotives were adopted in a number of countries, and they are still used in many cities and on some high-speed lines. Long-distance railway lines, however, are usually powered by diesel-electric locomotives.

The First Railways

The first trains were built to move goods – usually coal – and in most cases they were little more than carts fitted with special wheels, which allowed them to be guided along a track. Loads were transported in wagons with four wheels running along wooden guides, or planks. A peg was secured to the base of the wagon which fitted neatly into the gap between the planks, ensuring that the wagon remained on the tracks. Later railways had raised edges on the tracks to stop the wheels slipping off. Others had smooth rails, and the wheels themselves had a ridge at each side to keep them on the tracks.

Trains used in coal mines, or 'collieries', normally travelled downhill with their loads, often bringing coal to the rivers where it would be transported to its final destination by boat. Loaded coal wagons were called 'chaldrons', and they would roll along, controlled by a 'brakeman', who sat on or in the wagon.

The first self-propelled trains, those that were not powered by people but by special machinery on board, were driven by steam locomotives. Although the technology for steam engines was invented in 1712, it was not until the early nineteenth century that the first successful steam-powered railway locomotives were designed. The first self-propelled train in the United States of America was the 'scow'. This was really a type of boat and was created in 1804. The scow could travel on wheels under its own steam. When it reached water, the wheels were removed to enable it to continue its journey across the water.

The Steam Age

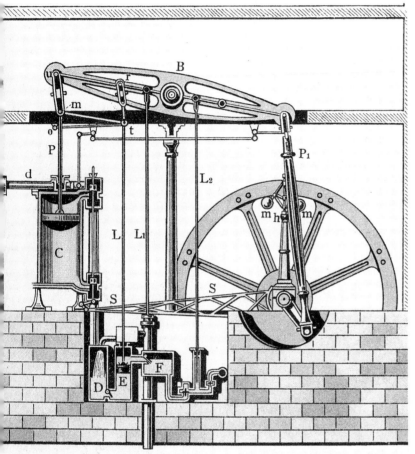

The first steps in steam engine design were made by two Englishmen: Thomas Newcomen in 1712, and James Watt in 1769. Basic railway lines were in use before this time, but the invention of the steam engine meant that they became far more widely used.

Britain was the birthplace of the steam locomotive. This is an engine powered by steam that is used to propel a wheeled vehicle on rails.

The steam engines that were used to power locomotives worked on a simple idea: when water is heated, it turns into steam. Steam expands until it reaches as much as 1,600 times its original volume. In a small space, such as an engine cylinder, this increase in volume creates pressure which is used to force 'pistons' back and forth. These pistons turn the driving wheels, which make the train move forward. Steam that has been used is then released from the chimney in 'puffs'.

The first steam locomotive was built in 1804 by Richard Trevithick for the Penydarren Iron Works in Wales. It was able to haul quite a big load (25 tons) but was too heavy for the track, so it was not very practical. His design could, however, be reproduced in smaller versions, which would be light enough to travel along the tracks without crushing them. Trevithick's locomotive pulled a four-wheeled carriage around a circular track and was the first steam locomotive to run in London, but it was another 25 years before locomotives began to be used widely.

Englishman George Stephenson built the engine 'Locomotion' for the Stockton and Darlington Railway, which was opened in 1825. This engine was large and powerful – its boiler had a capacity more suitable for 'freight' (transported goods, such as coal and wood) than for passenger service. Stephenson believed that steam locomotives were the way forward for the railways. This earned him the nickname 'Father of the Railways'. In 1823, together with his son Robert, he began to build steam locomotives for Britain and the rest of the world.

By 1829, Robert Stephenson had built the 'Rocket', which is thought by many to be the forerunner of the modern locomotive. The Rocket was completely self-sufficient; it carried coal to heat the boiler and a water supply to create steam. Later steam locomotives, such as 'Ellerman Lines' and the 'Mallard', worked in much the same way as the Rocket, although on a much larger scale.

The first successful steam locomotive to be built in the United States of America was the 'Best Friend' of Charleston, which entered service in 1830 and was used to operate the first steam railway service (railroad) in the US.

The crew of a locomotive consisted of a driver and a fireman. The driver controlled the locomotive using the regulator (also called a 'throttle'), reverser and brake. He was able to control the speed of the train while observing the signals and the speed limits on the track. The fireman was required to keep a good supply of steam by stoking the fire and ensuring that there was plenty of water in the boiler. It normally took about three hours for the crew to create enough steam to make a locomotive move.

By the mid-nineteenth century, the steam locomotive was being used world-wide, and its basic design remained almost unchanged until the invention of diesel-electric and electric locomotives signalled the end of the age of steam.

The First Modern Railways

EXPRESS GALOP
PAR
CH. D'ALBERT.

The first successful railway lines were those built in countries that were becoming more and more industrial, such as Britain, France and the US.

The opening of the first modern railway in England in 1830 created a great deal of interest around the world. People from many countries travelled to Britain to see and travel on it.

By the mid-nineteenth century, railroads had proved themselves to be much better than earlier forms of transport, such as turnpikes (or 'tollroads'), canals and steamboats. Later, as industrial development reached Asia, Africa, South America and Australia, railroads appeared on those continents. By the early years of the twentieth century, nearly 1,440,000 km (900,000 miles) of railway track had been built across the world.

Following the work of British inventor-engineers, the first railways appeared in the US during the late 1820s. In 1827, traders in Baltimore, Maryland, used the Baltimore & Ohio Railroad in order to increase trade with the western states. In 1829, the Delaware & Hudson Canal and Railroad Company purchased a British-built locomotive, the 'Stourbridge Lion', but found it too heavy for their track. On Christmas Day, 1830, the South Carolina Railroad began a passenger service on a 9.6 km (6 mile) stretch of track with the US-built 'Best Friend' of Charleston, becoming the first railroad in the nation to use steam power in regular service.

The first steam-operated railway in Germany was opened in 1835, and it ran between Nuremberg and Furth on an 8 km (5 mile) line. The locomotive, called 'Der Adler', was built in Britain.

Freight Trains

The first trains were developed to carry freight, and it was many years before carriages were built to transport people. Freight trains were widely used after the steam locomotive was invented and they became the fastest and most efficient way of transporting goods across countries around the world. By the end of the 1930s, the diesel-electric locomotive proved faster and more economical than steam, and within 20 years most freight trains were pulled by diesel engines.

The first trains could not travel faster than 50 km/h (30 mph) because their brakes were not very good and they could not stop easily. Most freight trains pulled wagons that did not have their own brakes. The only way to slow the train down was to apply the brake on the locomotive, and the guard's hand brake in the 'brake van'.

Modern freight trains are fitted with air brakes that can be operated by the driver. This means that they can safely travel at speeds of around 100 km/h (62 mph).

In the mid-nineteenth century, US freight cars tended to be of three types: the open-top car, the boxcar and the flatcar, each being able to carry no more than 10 tons. European freight cars have increased only slightly in size, while the capacity of American cars has expanded much more.

Among the types of freight cars most commonly used in the US are open hopper cars (mainly used for hauling coal), covered hopper cars (for grain and other bulky goods), tank cars (for hauling chemicals and other liquids) and flat cars, which can carry containers or highway truck trailers 'piggyback' and on which multi-level racks for carrying motor cars can be mounted.

Passenger Trains

The first public railways in the 1830s were operated with steam locomotives, carrying trains for both passengers and freight. Travel by railway, however, was quite crude by today's standards.

By the late 1830s, US trains were made up of elongated cars with double seats on either side of a central aisle. They could hold 40–50 people, and were similar in basic design to those of the mid-twentieth century. In contrast, many British and European passenger carriages consisted of several six- to eight-seat compartments with a corridor to one side.

Maison.

Signaux.

Télégraphe.

Sac.

Diable.

Sacoche.

Couverture.

Sleeping cars were introduced into the US by the 1860s, but they appeared in Britain only after 1870. Over the next 25 years electric lighting, steam heat and 'vestibules' (flexible, covered passageways between carriages) were being added to first-class passenger trains.

THE EXCURSION TRAIN CALOP

BY
FRANK MUSGRAVE.
LONDON: BREWER & Cº 23, BISHOPSGATE ST WITHIN.

In the first passenger trains, travellers were given the option of three different 'classes' of accommodation – first, second and third class – and the comfort of each one was very different. First-class accommodation had smaller, more private compartments with glass windows, padded seats, plenty of leg room and usually had easy access to a lavatory. Second class tended to be an open carriage with seats, but often with no heat or corridors to allow trips to the lavatory. Third-class carriages normally had no seats and passengers had to suffer periods of cold and rain, as there was no protection. In Britain, the second class disappeared fairly soon, as more people began to travel on railways, and third class became much more comfortable.

Electric Trains

Late in the nineteenth century, steam locomotive power was challenged by electric locomotives, both in Europe and in America. The first electric trains took their power from overhead cables, while others took power from a third 'live' (electric) rail on the track. Electric locomotives were quieter, faster and easier to run, although it was very expensive to turn existing railway lines into electric lines. Like diesels, electric trains use electric motors to drive the wheels but, unlike diesels, the electricity is generated externally at a power station and runs along overhead wires or a 'live' rail.

The first electric railway was designed in 1879 by German engineer Werner von Siemens. This locomotive could carry 30 passengers at a speed of 6.5 km/h (4 mph). In the US, the Baltimore & Ohio and the New York, New Haven & Hartford lines had successfully installed short, electrified routes about 6 km (3.75 miles) long by the turn of the century.

Electricity was soon used to create power for lines such as the under-ground, rapid transit systems and city links around the world. Some of the fastest trains today are powered by electricity, including Japan's Shinkansen and France's TGV (trains à grande vitesse).

Because they do not carry their own power-generating equipment, electric trains are not as heavy as other locomotives and can accelerate more quickly, making them most suitable for routes with many stops, such as underground trains in cities. Simpler electric trains are designed to perform special duties, such as moving passengers between terminals at airports.

Today, most railroads in industrial countries use either electric or diesel locomotives. Steam is still quite widely used, however, in many less-developed countries in Africa, Asia, and South America. As diesel locomotives have become more popular, electrified sections of railroads have also become more rare.

Diesel Power

The diesel engine was invented in the 1890s by Rudolf Diesel, a German mechanical engineer. The invention of the diesel locomotive made the operating of railways much more efficient.

The first diesel-electric locomotive was used by the Central Railroad of New Jersey in the mid-1920s. Early diesel locomotives like the Union Pacific were more expensive to build than steam locomotives, but were more efficient and cheaper to run, particularly when oil was plentiful.

The Deltic diesel-electric locomotive was built in 1956 and it was the most powerful locomotive in the world. The Deltics replaced the powerful streamlined steam locomotives of the Mallard type on the East Coast main line between London and Edinburgh in 1961.

Diesel locomotives are electric locomotives that carry their own power source. One main difference between diesel and electric is that the power cannot be applied directly to the wheels. Therefore, energy must be converted by using electricity. As a result, most diesel trains are known as 'diesel electrics'.

The diesel engine works by drawing air into cylinders and compressing it to increase its temperature. A small quantity of diesel fuel is then injected into the cylinders. This reacts with the air causing 'combustion', or burning, which drives the generator to produce electricity. This electricity is then fed to motors connected to the wheels.

During and after the Second World War, many trains were converted to diesel power. By 1952, the number of diesel locomotives was greater than that of steam locomotives.

Underground Trains

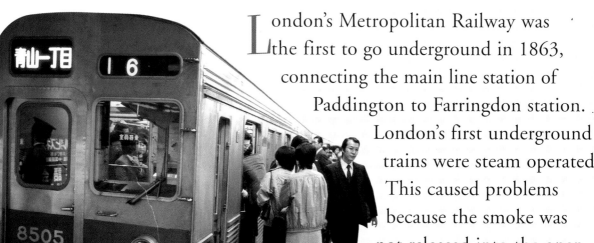

London's Metropolitan Railway was the first to go underground in 1863, connecting the main line station of Paddington to Farringdon station. London's first underground trains were steam operated. This caused problems because the smoke was not released into the open air as it was above ground, but was caught in the confined space.

At the end of the nineteenth century, due to the development of railways that were run by electricity, underground systems in London, Paris and Berlin were expanded. Boston built the first US 'subway' – the American term for the underground – in 1897, initially with streetcars instead of trains. New York City opened its first permanent subway in 1904 and for the next 40 years it continued to enlarge its subway system by increasing the amount of track and replacing its above-ground railroads with subways. In 1900, the underground railway opened in Paris and was called the 'Metro'. The Japanese underground railway opened in Tokyo in 1927, and is now one of the largest and busiest systems in the world, carrying millions of commuters each day in overcrowded trains.

Almost every major capital city in the world has built an underground train system since 1945. These railways are fast and help to reduce congestion in the streets above.

Some of the best underground railway lines include the Mexico City underground, which runs through suspended tunnels that can absorb shocks from earthquakes; the quiet and efficient Montreal subway, which uses rubber tyres on its trains; and the Hong Kong subway, the first fully air-conditioned underground railway.

Overhead Railways

The overhead or 'elevated' railway is a system that runs on a track built above street level, or which hangs beneath rails fixed to overhead structures. Trains usually have from two to ten carriages; station platforms are placed at the floor level of the carriages; and the carriages have several doors on each side for fast loading and unloading of passengers.

Quick and efficient transportation in large cities has been necessary since the middle of the nineteenth century. To ease congestion on the streets, London built underground railways. New York City found this more difficult, as the earth was made of solid rock. To solve this problem, they decided to build elevated railroads, opening the first line from Battery Place to Cortlandt Street along Greenwich Street in 1868.

Small steam locomotives were used for moving the first overhead trains. Beginning in the 1890s, electricity was used to run the elevated railroads which made them much cleaner. Elevated railway cars that run along tracks were – and still are – powered by electricity drawn from a third rail running alongside the tracks. Electricity reaches a motor that turns the driving wheel of the car. Speed is controlled by the operator.

Trains that do not run along the ground are divided into two types: 'suspended', where the train hangs under a rail or rails, or 'straddle', where the train fits over a single rail.

Suspended trains have wheels that are securely fitted on to the rails. Trains that straddle a single rail, called 'monorails', are balanced and guided by side panels on either side of the rail. The idea for a monorail was developed in the late nineteenth century, but it was not used until the 1960s.

Record-Breakers

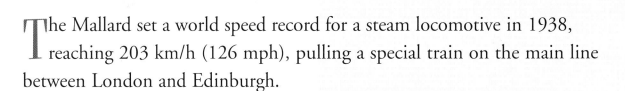

Trains, like most forms of transport, are always being designed to run faster, and there has been a great deal of competition between countries around the world to build the fastest train.

The first steam engines to run at 161 km/h (100 mph) were those used on the 'Hiawatha' service between Chicago and Minneapolis/St Paul in the US. This service holds the world record for the fastest-ever regular service run between two stations using steam power.

The Mallard set a world speed record for a steam locomotive in 1938, reaching 203 km/h (126 mph), pulling a special train on the main line between London and Edinburgh.

In 1893, the New York Central Railroad's steam locomotive No. 999 was the first steam train to go faster than 100 mph (161 km/h).

The Japanese first ran their famous 'bullet' train in 1964 – the Shinkansen. The train can go at a speed of 258 km/h (160 mph).

The French completed their train à grand vitesse (TGV) in 1981. Before a second line was opened in 1990, a more modern TGV train set a world speed record of 515.5 km/h (320 mph).

The newest train design, the 'Maglev' (magnetic levitation train), does not have wheels or rails, but instead it glides silently over a raised track, or 'guideway'. In Germany, a Maglev can speed around a 25 km (15.5 mile) track at 300 km/h (186 mph).

High-Speed Steam Trains

The Mallard, a steam locomotive, was designed by Sir Nigel Gresley, a British engineer. It was built in 1938 and set a world speed record in the first year that it ran.

One of the most famous express steam trains was the 'Flying Scotsman', which travelled 633 km (393 miles) between London and Edinburgh. This service was a landmark in the history of rail travel because of its speed.

The Best Friend of Charleston was the first commercial locomotive built in the US. It pulled a passenger train from Charleston over the 9.7 km (6 miles) of completed line of the South Carolina Railroad on Christmas Day, 1830. The short trip by the four-ton locomotive was the first scheduled run of a steam-powered railroad train in America. After several months of successful operation, the locomotive exploded when the engine's fireman tied down the safety valve of the boiler because the noise bothered him.

The Rocket was the early English locomotive, built by George and Robert Stephenson, that won the Rainhill trials, a competition sponsored by the Liverpool & Manchester Railway in 1829. By winning the competition the Rocket proved its reliability and convinced the sponsoring railway of the practicality of steam locomotive power. The Rocket completed the trials with an average speed of 24 km/h (15 mph) and a maximum of 47 km/h (29 mph).

High-Speed Diesels

One of the first successful high-speed diesel trains was the Burlington Zephyr, which ran along the Burlington route in the US. It travelled 1609 km (1000 miles), from Chicago to Denver in the mid-1930s. In 1935, it set a world record for going at an average speed of 134 km/h (83.3 mph), which is still a record for rail speed on a long journey.

The Deltic diesel-electric locomotive replaced express steam locomotives, and travelled at speeds of up to 160 km/h (100 mph). It was first built in 1956, and quickly became one of the most powerful trains in the world.

The Trans-Europe-Express (TEE) linked major European cities with a luxury express service. This service was fast, reliable, comfortable and first-class only.

A nother high-speed diesel train that carried passengers was the 'Super Chief' which first ran from Dearborn Station in Chicago in 1936. It was a luxury train made up of nine carriages called 'Pullman cars'. The train ran every week and reduced the time it took to get from Chicago to Los Angeles to just over 39 hours.

High-Speed Electric Trains

The TGV (train à grande vitesse) is a French electric high-speed train that was introduced in 1983. It has to travel at a speed of up to 274 km/h (170 mph) along a very steep route. The train mainly runs on specially built 'dedicated' tracks, which means that they are not used by any other kind of train. A TGV is made up of eight carriages with an electric locomotive at each end. The TGV is pulled by powerful electric locomotives, which are designed to allow the trains to keep going at a high speed, even when the

track is steep. The newer 10-car TGV trains are powered by electric locomotives that are at both the front and back of the train. Computers on the train control the brakes and the signals.

The Japanese 'bullet-train' uses the very latest technology. It began to run on 1 October 1964 to mark the start of the first Olympic Games in Asia, which were held in Tokyo. The first line it ran along was between Tokyo and Osaka and was 515 km (320 miles) long.

A 160 km (100 mile) extension to this line was completed in 1972 and ran from Osaka to Okayama. The final section – which was 393 km (244-miles) long – opened in 1975. Other lines, completed in 1982, run north of Tokyo.

The Maglev

The Maglev (magnetic levitation train), was designed to work without the use of a steel track or wheels. It glides silently over a raised track, or 'guideway'. It is held a few inches above this guideway by a magnetic field. Engineers have been testing the idea of a train without wheels or a track for several years.

The Germans' system uses 'electromagnets', magnets surrounded by a coil of wire through which electricity can pass. These are fixed underneath the train near the edge of the guideway. When an electric current flows through the magnets they are drawn towards a steel rail on the underside of the guideway, and the train is lifted by the force. In Germany, a Maglev speeds around a 25-kilometre (6-mile) track at 300 km/h (186 mph).

These Maglevs are still being researched, and some of the problems with them have not yet been solved. Engineers are working hard on them, though, because when they do work properly, they are the perfect train. As they have no moving parts, they do not wear out and no maintenance is required. They are ideal trains to have in cities as they do not create any pollution and make virtually no noise.

In Britain, a Maglev train service opened in Birmingham in the 1980s, running for 620 m (2,034 ft) between the airport to Birmingham's International Railway System. Maglev trains are being developed around the world to travel greater distances, and to run at very high speeds.

Future Trains

New types of trains and tracks are constantly being developed, even though rail travel has become much less popular recently due to cars and aeroplanes.

New high-speed railway lines are being built, and because of this, rail travel is making a comeback, especially in Europe. The success of France's TGV has encouraged countries such as Germany, Italy and Spain to run trains at speeds of around 250 km/h (150 mph). These trains now carry a great deal of railway traffic in western Europe, and there are plans to build more high-speed railway lines.

The Channel Tunnel between the UK and the Continent opened in 1994. Special electric 'Eurostar' trains began running from London to Paris and to Brussels. This tunnel has made the time it takes to get from London to Paris or Brussels very short. The 'Eurostar' makes the channel crossing in less than 35 minutes, and the journey from London to central Paris takes just under three hours.

British High Speed Trains now run on rehabilitated track, old tracks that have been modified to cope with the new trains. 'Tilt' trains, used a lot in Canada, travel at high speeds on normal railtracks but because of the sharp curves, they have special passenger coaches that tilt as they negotiate the turns, to help them balance and make them more comfortable.

Light rail transit systems, such as the Docklands Light Railway in London, provide frequent services in city centres and do not have drivers. They are operated by a computer from a central control room.

Further Information

Places to Visit

Bluebell Railway – Sheffield Park, Uckfield, East Sussex. Tel: 01825 722370.

The Discovery Museum – Blandford Square, Newcastle Upon Tyne, NE1 4JA. Telephone: 0191 232 6789.

Ironbridge Gorge Museum Trust – The Wharfage, Ironbridge, Telford, Shropshire, TF8 7AW. Telephone: 01952 433522.

London Transport Museum – 39 Wellington Street, Covent Garden, London, WC2E 7BB. Telephone: 0171 379 6344.

Museum of Transport – 1 Bunhouse Road, Glasgow, G3 8DP. Telephone: 0141 287 2720.

National Railway Museum – Leeman Road, York, YO26 4XJ. Telephone: 01904 621261.

Royal Museum of Scotland – Chambers Street, Edinburgh, EH1 1JF. Telephone: 0131 225 7534.

Science Museum – Exhibition Road, South Kensington, London, SW7 2DD. Telephone: 0171 938 8000.

Ulster Folk and Transport Museum – 153 Bangor Road, Coltra, Holywood, Co. Down, BT18 0AU, Ireland. Telephone: 01232 428428.

Further Reading

Eyewitness Guides: Train, Dorling Kindersley in Association with the National Railway Museum, 1992

Train Technology, Wayland, 1987

Ultimate Visual Dictionary, Dorling Kindersley, 1996

Usborne Young Scientist: Trains, Usborne Books, 1991

World's Transport: Rail Travel, by Alan Cooper, Wayland, 1992

Videos and CD Roms

DK Children's Dictionary, Dorling Kindersley

DK Children's Encyclopaedia, Dorling Kindersley (CD Rom)

DK Science Dictionary, Dorling Kindersley

Eyewitness Photographic Gallery: Trains, Dorling Kindersley

The Way Things Work, Dorling Kindersley

Picture Credits